52
Simple Ways
to Share
Your Faith

52 SIMPLE WAYS ·TO· SHARE YOUR FAITH

Roberta Hromas

A Division of Thomas Nelson Publishers
Nashville

To

My dear husband, Les,
who has lived a holy, honest faith
since childhood.
We have both been blessed to have had
great parents of faith
and doubly blessed to see our
children and grandchildren join us in living
so that every act is a sharing of faith
and every breath is a praise to God.

Copyright © 1991 by Roberta Hromas

Published in Nashville, Tennessee, by Oliver-Nelson Books, a division of Thomas Nelson, Inc., Publishers, and distributed in Canada by Lawson Falle, Ltd., Cambridge, Ontario.

Unless otherwise noted, the Bible version used in this publication is THE NEW KING JAMES VERSION. Copyright © 1979, 1980, 1982, Thomas Nelson, Inc., Publishers.

Printed in the United States of America.

Library of Congress Cataloging-in-Publication Data

Hromas, R. P.
   52 simple ways to share your faith / Roberta Hromas.
        p.   cm.
   ISBN 0-8407-9616-1
   1. Witness bearing (Christianity)   I. Fifty-two ways to share your faith.   II. Title.
BV4520.H76   1992
248'.5—dc20   92-1237
                                               CIP

1 2   3   4   5   6 — 97   96   95   94   93   92

• Contents

MAKING A PUBLIC STATEMENT

IN TIMES OF DIFFICULTY

CREATING CELEBRATIONS

MOVING INTO A FAITH-BASED CONVERSATION

• Introduction

Sharing your faith with others actually affords you the greatest opportunity of your life. As you share your faith, you increase your faith in God for a fruitful life now. You also build a reward for yourself in a glorious eternity with Christ Jesus. The greatest rewards of sharing your faith with others return to you.

We are called and challenged by Jesus Christ to be people of good words and good works—men and women who proclaim the good news of Jesus Christ in both word and deed. We are called to be light in a dark world.

In order to share our faith with others, we must catch a glimpse of their hearts—their motivations, hurts, needs, and purposes. We must begin to see them as the Lord Jesus sees them.

These 52 ways to share your faith have all been put to the test of everyday life and have brought proven results. I pray that your faith will begin to pervade every area of your life and provoke you to holy action. The consequences are His.

Major Events

1 • Birthdays

Birthdays are a good time to say, *"You are important to me and to God."*

In a birthday card or handwritten note on your own choice of stationery, take a few seconds to write a personal note of blessing or thanksgiving to God, such as:

I'm so grateful to the Creator for sending you to this earth and for the many talents and gifts He has given to you. I thank God for the privilege to know you.

Birthdays are a time when many people need to feel special. You can bring joy to them by writing a short note, saying,

Your presence here is important to me. I thank God that He arranged for us to live in the same area.

It is a special pleasure to be with you—your smile, your acceptance, and your care are noticed and appreciated. I pray on this day you will know the

depth and height of the Lord's love and care for you.

Birthday Blessings For a birthday party, suggest that everyone present give a word of blessing to the one who is being honored.

- Abundant peace and joy
- Overflowing prosperity
- Good health
- Your heart's desire

Have one person write each blessing on a card, along with the name of each person giving the blessing, and give the cards to the guest of honor at the party's end.

A "basket of blessings" is an excellent group gift, especially when the blessings are placed in an attractive container such as a crystal bowl, a brass planter, or a decorative box or basket.

A Special Birthday Bible A birthday is always a good time to give a Bible to a new acquaintance who does not have one. Write in it: "The message in this book is the greatest gift that I've ever received, and when I thought about what the best gift might be that I could give you, I knew it had to be this book."

2 • Christmas

Christmas is perhaps the easiest time of year to share your faith with a stranger. When the whole world is, theoretically at least, celebrating the birth of the One you know as Savior and Lord, how much easier it is to share the *reality* of His life.

As you purchase gifts and decorations during the holiday season, take time to say to the clerk who is helping you, *"I'm buying this to celebrate the birthday of my Lord!"*

A Carol Sing Consider inviting your neighbors and friends to an old-fashioned carol sing, followed by refreshments or a potluck dinner. Feel free, as host or hostess, to begin or end the party by sharing what the Christmas season means to you, having a guest read the story of Christmas from Luke 2:1–20, or praying for the safety, health, and spiritual well-being of those who are present.

A Special Church Service This season is also an especially good time to invite a friend and her entire family to go to church with you—for the Christmas pageant, the Advent choir presentation, the Christmas Eve communion service, or the children's program. Arrange a time of fellowship after-ward. Ask each person, young and old alike, to share his favorite part of the Christmas story.

Tree Decorating Party   Have a Christmas tree decorating party and invite your neighbors. Cut out, make, and hang tree ornaments that are symbols related to the Scriptures and have each person take home a favorite. String popcorn and cranberries and talk about the origin of various holiday traditions. What a wonderful time of shar-ing this can be as you explore the meaning of the season in a casual, informal way.

The Story of Christmas   Christmas is an ex-cellent time to give to each of your neighbors' chil-dren a book that tells the Bible's Christmas story. (It could be part of a larger book of Bible stories.) You may even want to present them with children's Bibles.

3 • Thanksgiving

Thanksgiving is a custom rooted in Jewish history. The original thanksgiving feast, called the Feast of Tabernacles or Sukkoth, has been celebrated by the Jews for thousands of years. The Puritans, who were ardent students of Jewish customs, were among those who observed the Feast of Tabernacles on a regular basis.

The Feast of Tabernacles is the only Jewish feast to which Gentiles are invited. As the Thanksgiving season approaches, ask the Lord whom He would like for you to invite to your table—to whom He desires for you to show His love.

A Thanksgiving Pageant Host a neighborhood Thanksgiving pageant. Invite the neighborhood children to your home for several Saturdays before Thanksgiving to write a play, make costumes, and rehearse. In preparing for the pageant, share with the children the historical origins of Thanksgiving, the meaning of a thankful heart, and the faith of many of our nation's founders. Hold the pageant the night before Thanksgiving and close with a special thanksgiving prayer read by the children and their audience in unison.

Around Your Table   You can share your faith around your Thanksgiving table in a number of ways:

- *Write Scripture verses as placecards.* Have each person read his or her placecard before or after the meal. Choose verses about our thankfulness to God, such as

    Psalm 106:1   Colossians 1:12–14
    1 Corinthians 15:57   Colossians 1:16–17
    2 Corinthians 2:14   Revelation 4:9
    2 Corinthians 9:15   Revelation 11:17

- *Write a Thanksgiving prayer* and put a copy of it on each plate so that you may all read it aloud together before your meal.
- *Ask the children to write specific things for which they are thankful*—one item per card. Let them decorate the cards with crayons or stickers, and then put one card at each place. Before the blessing for the meal, ask several people to read the cards at their places. During the meal ask the adults, "What would you have written on your card?"

4 • Mother's Day and Father's Day

Do you have friends who recently became parents? Remember them in a special way on Mother's Day and Father's Day.

Send a card or write a note. Take the opportunity to rejoice with them that their baby is a gift from God. Include a special prayer:

Heavenly Father, I ask You to give my friends Your wisdom as they raise their baby. May they always be aware that You knew their baby and its purpose on this earth even before they did. Help them to show their baby Your love and to raise their child to know Your Word.

Adopt a Mother or Father Late on the Saturday before the Sunday holiday, buy unsold flowers at discounted prices. Take them to women or men who have befriended you. Add a little note: "Thank you for being a second parent. Even though our lives here will last only a few years, I have the hope that we will spend all eternity together."

Spiritual Mother or Father   Is there someone in your life whom you consider to be a spiritual
mother or father—someone who first shared the
gospel with you, led you to the Lord, or taught the
Bible to you? Has someone mentored or counseled
you, helped you establish your home on God's
principles, or encouraged you in your walk with
the Lord? Remember those people on Mother's
Day or Father's Day. Let them know how special
they have been to you. Your notes to them will be a
witness to those around them.

Don't fail to express God's love and your love to
your own mother and father. Build each parent's
faith with a note: "I thank my heavenly Father for
you, my earthly parent. I thank you for each caring
expression toward me. I honor you on your day!"

5 • Graduation

Graduations are transitions in the lives of young people—and, increasingly so, those who aren't so young. Graduation is an excellent time to say or write to a graduate:

Times may be changing in your life, but my love for you isn't. The Lord has given me a touch of His love for you—the kind of love that doesn't change and doesn't diminish over time.

Graduation is also a good time to point toward the future:

My prayer is that you will walk forward with renewed faith in God, who has only the best plans for your life and who makes all these things possible.

I can hardly wait to see how the Lord's full plan and purpose for your life unfold. It will be marvelous.

You are a treasure of heaven entrusted to fulfill God's exciting purposes for your place on the earth. I encourage you to do and be all He is calling you to do and be.

Sometimes your greatest example of Christian love to the graduate is simply to attend the graduation ceremony.

- In honoring a graduate—whether from kindergarten or a Ph.D. program—you are expressing Christlike love and concern not only for that person but for his entire family.
- A graduation marks a beginning in the life of each family member, so take this opportunity to express joyous anticipation of the future with the entire family.
- Write a note to the parents or the spouse who helped your friend reach this milestone in her life.

Take the opportunity of a graduation to show others that this is how a Christian cares.

6 · Weddings and Engagements

As a couple prepare to be married, their thoughts often turn to the more serious, spiritual aspects of life. Take the opportunity of a wedding or an engagement celebration to share from the Scriptures.

Add a verse of Scripture to a card:

I pray that your love may abound still more and more in knowledge and in all discernment (Phil. 1:9).

I pray that your "hearts may be . . . knit together in love" (Col. 2:2).

The Lord make you to increase and abound in love one to another, and to all (1 Thess. 3:12).

A Word Study   Give the engaged couple or the newlyweds a card or note in which you have listed a series of Scriptures, with the introduction: *"I trust you will have a precious time together as you search the Scriptures to discover God's desire for your marriage."*

Include on your list such passages as:

Genesis 2:24	1 Corinthians 7:1–5
Proverbs 18:22	1 Corinthians 13
Hosea 2:19	Colossians 3:12
Matthew 25:34–40	Hebrews 13:4
Luke 6:31–35	

A Wedding Prayer   Write a prayer of your hopes for the soon-to-be-married couple.

Heavenly Father, I pray that You will be the center of the home that is about to be established by _____ and _____. Let them love and serve You together all the days of their lives. May their home be filled with peace, laughter, and caring love. May their home be a secure refuge from the world.

May they nurture each other in their understanding of You and help each other to love You more each day.

May they experience exceeding joy in the beauty of the married life they share. May their thankfulness to God be expressed daily by tender care for each other.

May Your blessing be upon them now and forever.

Amen.

7 • Birth or Adoption of a Baby

When you celebrate the arrival of a friend's new child, you touch the very heart of that family.

Give a copy of the Bible or New Testament with the child's name imprinted on it   A number of quality children's Bibles are available in a variety of bindings that can be easily and attractively personalized. Inscribe a message to the child on the inside: "May this be your guide for life" or "May you come to know the joy and peace of God in your life."

Give a nameplate   A number of styles are now available, and some give the spiritual meaning of the child's name. Along with your gift, tuck in a short note: "Your name is precious to me and to the Lord; may you call on His name even as He calls yours."

Give any item that you have personalized with the child's name or initials   Birth is an excellent time to give gifts that are monogrammed or imprinted with the child's name. Call attention to the fact that this child

- is unique—one of a kind. God never does anything twice in exactly the same way.
- has been created by God.
- has a divine purpose on the earth.
- is loved.

If the child has been named in honor of a parent, grandparent, or someone else you know, write a special letter to the child. Tell the child what you know about the person who shares his name. A similar letter is appropriate for a child with the same name as a Bible hero.

Give a living gift You can also plant a tree in honor of a child's birth, perhaps in a park near your church or even in Israel.* This gift provides an excellent opportunity for expressing your hope that the child will be "planted always by the rivers of living water."

---

* You can plant a tree in Israel by contacting the Jewish National Fund, 42 East 69th Street, New York, NY 10211. The cost is about $10 a tree, which includes a certificate that they will mail to your friend.

8 • Moving to a New Home or Apartment

A housewarming party is an excellent time to share your faith with a friend.

Welcome friends to their new home with a "party" that you bring with you. Have each person show up at your friends' new home with a dozen balloons and a small gift or dessert. Fill the house with festivity. Before you leave, have a time of prayer:

Heavenly Father, we ask that You make this home a haven of Your presence. Protect those who live here and all who enter as friends and guests. Bar evil from this place; let no harm come to this house or to those who dwell within it.

A Gift Basket Welcome a new neighbor with a gift basket, perhaps filled with a tin of brownies, a small houseplant, a map of the city, a welcoming brochure to your church, and a little box of "promise cards" with a note: "For your kitchen table."

Think back to your last move. What items did you need most in the first few days of unpacking and getting acquainted with a new city? Put these items in a "care package" for your new neighbors.

Housewarming Gifts   You can express your faith in a variety of ways through a housewarming gift, such as:

- a piece of needlework proclaiming "God bless this house."
- a work of calligraphy.
- candles, with a note: "For your first candlelit dinner in your new home."

Help with the Move   An extra pair of hands is nearly always welcome in a move—to gather boxes and packing material, to pack boxes, to unpack boxes, or to discard the boxes after the move. You can also wash dishes or watch the children. If professional movers haven't been hired, the family will appreciate everyone who can carry boxes and lend a hand with heavy furniture.

As you help do the work of the move, bring up topics related to the Bible and to your faith:

- *"Have you ever thought about what it would have been like to be one of the Israelites that Moses led out of Egypt to go to the Promised Land? They were moving all the time!"*
- *"I think I know better what the Bible means when it talks about all of us being sojourners through this life."*

9 • Easter

Easter is the time to invite everyone you know to go to church with you. No matter what your denomination, you'll likely find that your unchurched friends are more likely to accept an invitation to attend an Easter service than a regular Sunday service.

Plan to take your invited guests to brunch or lunch afterward, or plan a gathering in your own home. Having lunch not only adds value to your invitation, but it also gives you an opportunity to discuss questions they may have about the service or the sermon.

Sunrise Service In many cases your friends have never attended, or may never have even heard about, a sunrise service. Tell them, "Never been to one? It's an *adventure!* You ought to go to at least one sunrise service in your life. We'll pick you up at 5:30 A.M. on Easter Sunday."

Easter Musicals Many churches sponsor Easter musicals, pageants, or "passion plays." (A passion play is a theatrical production about the last few days of Jesus' life, usually beginning with the triumphant entry into Jerusalem on Palm Sunday and ending with His resurrection on Easter Sunday.) Invite your friends to attend one of these productions with you. Perhaps you can have dinner first or dessert following the performance.

Easter Basket Stuffer Do you have a godchild, grandchild, niece, nephew, or another special child that you normally remember with a small gift at Easter? Consider giving the child a small book that tells the true Easter story!

The Easter Parade Story As you talk about Easter with your friends, share with them the true story of how the Easter parade came to be. Immediately following the Sunday morning service, the parishioners of a large church adopted the custom of taking the Easter lilies that adorned their altar to the residents of a nursing home a few blocks away. Local residents began to gather to watch the church members in their finery march from the church to the nursing home with the lilies, and thus, the Easter parade was born. The original parade was an act of giving!

Good Friday Good Friday provides an excellent opportunity for you to witness to your business associates. If you work for an organization that doesn't close for Good Friday, consider requesting it as a vacation day. Tell your boss that you'd like to spend time in worship that day. Even if you don't take off the entire day, you may want to ask permission to leave work early or take a long lunch hour in order to attend a Good Friday service at a church near your workplace. Invite others to come with you if it is appropriate.

In Your Neighborhood

10 • New Neighbors Barbecue

If you have recently moved into a new neighborhood, invite your Christian friends over to a "new-house blessing" and invite your new neighbors to come, too. Don't compromise your faith or get on a soapbox. Be who you are. You have control in your own home. Be comfortable relating key aspects of your spiritual life with friends as you introduce them to a new neighbor, saying:

This is Doug and Beverly. They are a part of our Sunday school class. We attend (give name of church). Do you have a church home?

This is Joe. He and Edna were the first people we met when we moved to this city, and they were also the first ones who invited us to go to church with them.

Before dinner, ask one of your friends to pray a blessing over your meal and to include a blessing for your new home.

A party with your Christian friends provides an opportunity for witness on many fronts. Your neighbors will likely sense a difference in the language of those who attend the party and in the topics discussed among you. Use the get-together as an opportunity to let your choices of music and beverages be a witness, too.

- Let your neighbors leave your home knowing that they have Christians as neighbors.
- Let them leave with the feeling that they would like to be part of such a joyful group of people.
- Let them leave feeling loved and respected.

There's no time as easy as when you first move into the neighborhood to have this get-acquainted-with-your-neighbors party. Don't wait too long!

11 • Welcoming Tea

Has a close friend moved into a new neighborhood? Sponsor a tea on her behalf and invite both old friends and new neighbors.

Ask your friend to let you host the party in her new home with the full assurance that you, as the sponsor, will be responsible for preparing refreshments, sending invitations, planning a program, and cleaning up!

Before the Tea A week before the planned event, go door-to-door in your friend's new neighborhood or apartment complex and personally deliver invitations to the tea. This extra effort will give you an opportunity to meet your friend's new neighbors so that you will be able to welcome them to the tea.

If the neighborhood includes many women who work, you may want to make the tea a Saturday morning coffee hour instead.

Be true to your word—bring everything necessary for the party with you to your friend's new home: food, flowers, napkins, beverages.

During the Tea   Have each of the long-standing friends of your friend share an anecdote with the entire group that will let the new neighbors know, "You're fortunate to have this woman living in your neighborhood!"

Have one person pray a blessing over your friend and her new home during the event:

Heavenly Father, thank You for our friend and for her new home and neighborhood. We know that You are always with her and that her heart's desire is to have a home in which the name of Jesus is lifted up. We're grateful to You for giving her these neighbors, and we ask You to bless her as she shares her life with those in her neighborhood.

Be sure to greet each person who attends the tea with warmth and appreciation. Have each guest tell something about herself, how long she has lived in the neighborhood, or the most exciting event in the neighborhood's history.

Not only will your friend be established as a Christian in her new neighborhood—and as a person to whom others might turn in time of need—but you will be an example of Christ's love as you host such an event.

12 • Block Party

Have you been living in your neighborhood for some time but don't know all your neighbors? Have people moved in and out of your neighborhood in the last year or so?

Have a block party or an apartment building bash. Designate a meeting place that allows enough room for everyone to come—perhaps the community center or the clubhouse of your apartment complex. Or make it a true block party by blocking off a section of your street. (Be sure to get the city's permission in advance.) You provide the soft drinks.

Potluck or Cookout If you have a potluck dinner, make sure someone brings delicious desserts.

If you decide to have a cookout at one person's house, ask each family to bring meat and at least one other dish. Don't let the party become a burden to any one family. Be sure that everyone helps clean up.

You may hand out cards at the event that give your name, address, and telephone number, as

well as your church's name, address, and weekly
schedule.

Activities for Children   Plan activities for
the children—set up a volleyball net, croquet wick-
ets, or a Frisbee golf course.*

If you decide to have the event on a holiday (the
Fourth of July is a good day for an annual block
party), consider having a patriotic parade featuring
the neighborhood children and their pets.

Use this get-acquainted time to ask your neighbors where they attend church. If they don't have a
regular church home, invite them to attend with
you.

A block party will give you significant clues
about

- the needs in your neighborhood.
- those in your neighborhood who don't have a
  personal relationship with the Lord Jesus.
- those in your neighborhood who are not attending church and perhaps know very little
  about Jesus Christ.
- the prayer needs of those who live close to
  you.

---

* A Frisbee golf course works this way. Set up "holes" that are
about two feet in diameter. Then set up places where the players
will "tee off" for each hole. Keep track of how many tosses you have
to make to get at least half of your Frisbee into the designated hole.
You may want to have score cards and pencils available.

13 • Neighborly Giving

Be a giver. The more flowers you cut from your garden, the more the plants will grow back and blossom.

Your Garden Produce Freely share the produce from your vegetable garden, your flower garden, and your fruit trees. As you hand your neighbor a basket of homegrown tomatoes, include a mention of the Lord in a natural, unobtrusive way: "As far as I'm concerned, nothing tastes as good as a tomato vine-ripened by God. I hope you enjoy these."

Your Prayers In times of need, you may want to prepare a casserole for the family of someone who is ill in your neighborhood. As you deliver it, look for the opportunity to volunteer your prayers.

May Baskets May baskets of flowers, delivered on the first day of May, are a dying tradition in our nation. Bring it back to your neighborhood. Surprise your neighbors with a basket of flowers on their doorstep next May Day. Tuck in a Scripture about God's care for us. You may want to have your children decorate your Scripture message with drawings or stickers. Let them be a part of your May Day basket making and delivery.

Help Out Spend a Saturday helping someone in your neighborhood who needs assistance with a neglected yard. Trim branches, remove weeds, and rake leaves. Do it for the Lord. Take pleasure in carrying out His orders.

14 • Agape Feast

In the early days of the church, believers shared much of their lives together, far beyond an hour of worship on Sunday mornings. A key aspect of their community life was a tradition that came to be known as an "agape meal." (*Agape* is the Greek word used to describe God's love.)

You can host an agape feast, a potluck, in your own home, the community hall, or the recreation room at your apartment complex.

Speaker First, invite someone to be a guest speaker for the evening—perhaps a local athlete, a business executive, or a well-known person in your community who has made a public declaration of her faith. Let the speaker know that you'd like to invite a group of your friends, both churchgoers and nonchurchgoers, to hear a personal testimony. Many people are very willing, even eager, to share their stories in this way.

Ask groups of people to help you assemble folding chairs, card tables, and coffee makers; to call with invitations; to host the event; and to clean up. You'll also find it helpful to put a starting and ending time on your invitation, perhaps from 6:00 P.M. to 9:00 P.M. or from 7:00 P.M. to 10:00 P.M.

Then, invite your Christian friends and your neighbors, including those you would like to introduce to the love of the Lord. Try to have at least thirty people in attendance.

Agape feasts are especially good times to minister to children and to build up their faith.

Scripture As the guests arrive, give each person a verse of Scripture to read. Choose in advance verses that relate to a specific topic, such as prayer or God's love.

Sharing Make the time of eating an exciting event with open conversation. Then gather everyone together to sing from prepared songsheets. Introduce your speaker with her complete credentials to give authority to her testimony. Close with a brief prayer.

15 • Children's Club

One of the best ways to share your faith is to share Bible stories with your neighbors' children.

Start a neighborhood children's club that can meet at your home on a regular basis—perhaps once a month or once a week for several weeks during the summer. You might want to set aside Saturday mornings and provide this activity as an alternative to cartoons. Consider a two-hour time frame for refreshments, games or crafts, and a Bible story.

Having a children's gathering on Saturday morning gives your neighbors a "parent's time alone" and gives the children a chance to have fun with other children of various ages. Challenge the older ones to pray, read the Bible daily, and live the Christian life even if others do not. Give them a meaty Bible lesson.

When you invite the children, make certain that the parents know their children are going to hear a story from the Bible.

Several published programs are available to help you host such an event, for example:

- *5-Day Club*
- *Good News Club*
- *Release Times*
- *National Children's Prayer Network*

Have a handout, booklet, or printed prayer that tells the child—and his or her parents—what to do in order to have a personal relationship with Jesus Christ. You may also want to provide a simple three-step method for the parents:

One   To help your child become acquainted with the Bible, you can purchase a children's Bible storybook at a Christian bookstore and set aside at least one evening a week for reading a story to him.

Two   To help your child develop a relationship with God, pray with her each evening as she goes to bed. Pray for your child's safety during the night and for specific needs that she may have. Encourage your child to pray, too, verbalizing several things for which she is thankful.

Three   To lead your child into a personal relationship with the Lord Jesus, encourage him to pray:

God in heaven, thank You for sending Jesus to the earth to show me what You are like. Please forgive me for my sins and help me to do what is right in Your sight. I want to be Your friend forever and live with You in heaven someday. In Jesus' name I pray, Amen.

In the Normal
Course of Living

16 • Sharing with Loved Ones Far Away

Perhaps you live far away from your loved ones who don't love the Lord Jesus. You know that they aren't attending church, and they aren't likely to be reading their Bibles. What can you do?

Pray for Them You can—and must—pray for them. Ask the Lord to send others across their paths who will be open in sharing the gospel with them in a way that they will accept.

Use the Telephone Second, offer to pray for them by telephone, especially when they are facing a difficult decision, when they are ill or injured, when they have a friend who has been in an accident, or when they simply need a large dose of encouragement.

Ask for Insight Third, ask the Lord to give you insight into what you might share with them from His Word that will encourage them. As you read your Bible, be aware of verses that might uplift or affirm your family members.

Write   Fourth, write down the Scriptures that seem the most beneficial, and mail them with brief notes or letters.

Relate each Scripture passage to a particular problem or circumstance you know that person is facing:

> *When we heard, Craig, about the difficulties you are facing in the development of your new product line, we were reminded of James 1:5 in God's Word: "If any of you lacks wisdom, let him ask of God, who gives to all liberally and without reproach, and it will be given to him."*

For comfort in times of stress and dire need, suggest he read Psalm 121 or Psalm 91, or copy these psalms from your favorite version of the Bible and send them to him.

By sharing an encouraging word from the Lord, you are expressing love and planting a seed of faith. God's Word will not return void; it always bears fruit. Remember, too, that fruit rarely appears overnight.

17 • Sharing at the Office

The small plaque read: "There's no limit to what God can do if man doesn't care who gets the credit."

Those simple but profound words were read by hundreds of the most politically and socially powerful people in the world as they passed through the Oval Office during the eight years that Ronald Reagan served as president of the United States. That small plaque carried a powerful message!

Subtle Ways You can share your faith in profound and subtle ways in the workplace. Consider the following:

- *Desk or wall calendars with scriptural references*
- *Objects that include spiritual symbols*
- *Collected objects from the Holy Land*

Any object of beauty, of course, can be used to start a conversation about the Lord, who is the very embodiment of the "beauty of holiness."

The Key Idea The key idea in having spiritually meaningful objects in your workplace is this: let others do the asking.

- Don't display objects in order to manipulate others.
- Keep on display only those objects, symbols, and messages that are meaningful and inspirational to you.
- Let the Holy Spirit use them to pique the interest of others, and then freely share as others ask about them, telling what the objects mean to you not what you hope they will mean to them.

Remember the saying, "What you do speaks so loudly I can't hear what you say."

Keep the sharing of your faith open, honest, unmanipulative, and unobtrusive in the workplace. The Holy Spirit calls us to live in an orderly fashion (see Acts 21:24).

Make certain any objects that you have in your office are in good taste and in keeping with the decorum and protocol that your employer expects.

18 • Sharing as You Go

As you go about your daily life, scatter blessings just as Johnny Appleseed once scattered apple-seeds. Some will take root and grow; others won't. That is up to the Lord.

To the clerk or waitress who gives you excellent service, in addition to leaving a good tip you might say,

I ask the Lord to reward you for the good service you have given me.

At Christmastime, you might say,

May the Lord, whose birthday we're celebrating, bless you.

To the cab driver who tells you about his recent arrival in America, you might say,

I pray you will come to know God's blessings in this country, where even our money says, "In God We Trust."

To your child's teacher, you might say,

Thank you for helping my child this year. I pray that the Lord will use you in a special way in his life. May God reward you for your efforts as a teacher.

To the neighbor boy who mows your lawn,

I'm sure the Lord is pleased that you are helping to take such good care of His creation. God bless you!

Give encouragement, blessing, or thanks in the name of the Lord as you

- shop.
- eat in restaurants or fast-food places.
- take public transportation.
- conduct your personal business at the bank or post office.
- drop your clothes off at the dry cleaners and take your shoes in for repair.
- pay those who shampoo your carpets, fix your car, immunize your pet, trim your trees, clean your house, or service your air conditioning unit.
- walk out of the dentist's or doctor's office.
- leave the hotel lobby.

Take special note of each person who serves you. Jesus said that their service to you, as God's child, does not go unnoticed by the Father (see Matt. 10:40–41). That's all the more reason why we should take notice, too.

Your words, however brief, may be the only kindness those people receive all day. Your expression of thanks may be the only communication that builds them up, encourages them, and calls their attention to the Lord. Jesus said that even a cup of cold water given to a thirsty person in His name was a way of blessing and honoring Him (see Mark 9:41). Consider your words to be a cup of cold water to a spiritually parched world.

19 • Sharing with Fellow Shoppers

There are four principles to keep in mind as you share your faith with fellow consumers:

Identification First, look for a point of identification with someone near you. What about her attracts you or makes you feel a kinship with her? Zero in on a shared experience or common interest.

Conversation Second, don't be afraid to open a conversation. Trust the Spirit of Truth to inspire your thoughts. Don't allow yourself to become either discouraged or prideful with the results.

Affirmation Third, speak affirmation to the person. Say something to build him up or encourage him.

Key Response Fourth, look for a response that tells you that the Holy Spirit is using your words. People usually

- tear up (and sometimes begin to cry).
- "light up" and express their interest.

- linger, seeming to want to hear more.
- ask questions.

When those things happen, forge ahead to share the gospel. Share as much as the person is willing to receive.

Remember, you may well be the answer to someone else's prayer: "Lord, send someone across the path of my loved one."

20 • Sharing in the Mall Parking Lot

A good "anonymous" way to share your faith is to suggest to your youth leader that you and a group at your church do the publicity for a major musical or theatrical presentation already scheduled at your church.

Fliers Make up fliers—generally 8 1/2-by-11-inch—and have them duplicated on brightly colored paper. With today's easy access to computers, you can probably work with a couple of the young people to create an unusual design or invitation using computer graphics.

Be sure to include the date and the time, the place, the name of the presentation, and the names of any guest musicians or actors. It also helps to have the word *free* clearly visible. State somewhere on the flier the reason you think people should attend and that children and teenagers are invited to come, too. Add a promise from the Bible that can be cut out and kept.

Plan an Outing A week before the event, plan an outing for the entire youth group to a mall parking lot. Be sure to get permission to distribute the fliers from the mall's management office.

Before you go, discuss with the young people what to say if anyone should ask them what they are doing. Express the need for them to be enthusiastic about people attending the performance. Reassure them that they are inviting the community to a program that will be both inspirational and well done. Be sure they have all the details about the performance in case anyone asks them face-to-face for more information.

Have a time of prayer together that this bread you are "casting out on the waters" will result in people coming to know the Lord (see Eccles. 11:1). As you pray, mention those who are producing or presenting the program, and ask that the upcoming program will be one of the highlights of the entire year at church.

At the mall, put a flier under the windshield wiper of each car, section by section.

After you've distributed the fliers, you might want to treat everybody to ice cream.

21 • Praying the Phone Book

Join with others in your Sunday school class, Bible study group, or church in "praying the phone book."

Take a Page   Have each person take a page of the local directory—the one that serves the immediate community around your church. Pray for each name on your page over the course of a week or two. In an average four-column phone book, you'll probably have about 350 to 400 names per page. It will take you only ten minutes or so to pray for all the names in one column.

As you intercede for each family, pray that

- each non-Christian member of the family will be invited to attend a church service where the gospel of Jesus Christ will be preached in a way that is easy for him to understand and to accept.
- each person will experience the grace of God in a new and more powerful way in her life, and the Holy Spirit will plant in her a desire for freedom from sin.
- each unsaved person will come to know Jesus Christ as his personal Savior and Lord.

Call the Names As your church prepares for its traditional Christmas, Easter, or summer musical or pageant, call the names on your page of the phone book, and invite them to attend the special service. Each call will take you only sixty seconds, and since many people now have answering machines, you will probably be able to reach nearly everyone on your page if you call just one hour a day for a week. Simply say,

> *Hi, I'm a neighbor of yours,* [your name], *and I'd like to invite you to a special musical* [or theatrical] *presentation we're having at* [your church name] *on* [date] *at* [time]. *The program is entitled* [title], *and it's about* [brief description of program]. *The program is free, and I think your entire family would enjoy it. If you have young children, a nursery is available. If you'd like more information, you can call me back at* [your phone number] *or call the church at* [church phone number].

Try to make your calls at least a week before the program so that people will have time to make plans to attend.

Praying for the people of your community will make you more sensitive to their needs. They are part of your "Jerusalem, Judea, and Samaria." It's important to recognize them as potential neighbors in the eternal, heavenly city, the New Jerusalem.

22 • Turning Conflicts into Blessings

Many times we become frustrated at troublesome incidents that seem to occur unexpectedly as part of everyday life when these situations may well be part of the Lord's design to introduce us to those who need to hear His Word the most. It's up to us to decide how we will respond—and whether we will turn a potential conflict into an opportunity to share something about the Lord with others. Let's choose to share.

The parking lot at the mall was particularly full on that Saturday before Christmas. I had circled the lot several times, and I finally came across a car that was pulling out. To my surprise, as that car left, another car coming from the opposite direction sped into the space, missing the front of my car by only a few inches.

Opportunity I quickly prayed, "Lord, what shall I do about this?" and I decided that the Lord would want me to turn an unpleasant situation into an opportunity to share His love.

As two teenage boys got out of the car, I rolled

down the window and called to them, "May I speak with you for a moment?"

They rather sheepishly approached my car, and I told them, "Since I've been waiting for this space for some time, the Lord must have allowed this to happen so that we would have an opportunity to meet." I introduced myself and then asked the boys, "Do you know that God loves you?"

One of the boys blurted out, "Are you sure?"

"Oh, yes," I said. "Haven't you boys ever heard that before?"

One of the boys responded sincerely, "No, I haven't." The other said, "Yeah, I think I heard that once before when my grandmother took me to a Sunday school class when I was about seven years old."

Challenge I continued to ask them questions related to the gospel and was shocked to realize that these two teenagers, who had grown up in the United States, knew nothing of Jesus. I challenged them to find a Bible and read the book of Mark, telling them that it was written by a young man about their age. I also invited them to watch a Christian television program the next Sunday morning. I couched our discussion in these terms: "You really should know what's happening so you'll be in the know about the Christmas season."

23 • While Discussing Current Events

Current news events, especially news of conflicts in the Middle East, frequently cause people to speculate about the future. You can use such discussions as opportunities to share what you know about the Bible's view of time and eternity.

- Say that **the Bible does not speculate.** It conveys absolute truth about the future. It tells us with certainty what *will* happen someday, as humanity runs its course against God's timetable.
- Say that **the Bible calls us to live "one day at a time"—to live in the present.** Those who live in the future are subject to fear, and the Bible warns that men's hearts will fail as a result (see Luke 21:26).
- Say that **the Bible tells us what we must do to have eternal life.** Jesus summed it up with these words: "For God so loved the world that He gave His only begotten Son, that whoever believes in Him should not perish but have everlasting life" (John 3:16).
- Say that **the Bible tells us how we are to live on this earth.** You can always refer a

person to Psalms and Proverbs as a "short course" from the Manual of Life, the wisdom of God Almighty.

- Say that **God desires for us to have peace even in the midst of extreme chaos and destruction.** Jesus said in His conclusion to a lengthy statement about future difficult times, "These things I have spoken to you, that in Me you may have peace. In the world you will have tribulation; but be of good cheer, I have overcome the world" (John 16:33). We can always assure those around us that even though times may be difficult, we can experience inner peace by having a relationship with the Lord Jesus.

In discussions with your friends, encourage them to look up these issues or topics in the Bible. Show them how to use a concordance for word studies on themes such as money, war, famine, Israel, and earth.

When current events cause people to ask you about the nature of humanity and God's relationship to wars and catastrophes, suggest that they read God's eternal truth on these subjects for themselves.

Use uncertain times as opportunities to interject faith, times of doubt and questioning as opportunities to interject assurance and hope, and times of worry as opportunities to interject peace.

24 • Speaking Up Against Evil

Although no social researcher is going to claim that our TV-viewing or reading habits actually *cause* an increase in crime and immorality in our nation, many agree that the *correlations* are high between the viewing of violence and acts of violence, between the viewing of immoral behavior and sexual responses, and between the availability of pornography and the increase in sexual crimes.

One of the best ways to share your faith is to take a stand against evil. God's Word admonishes us to abstain from even the appearance of evil (see 1 Thess. 5:22), to give no place to the devil (see Eph. 4:27), and to abhor what is evil (see Rom. 12:9).

- **Refuse to participate, even vicariously, in violence and sexual immorality.** Don't watch programs that portray murder, rape, fornication, adultery, and other criminal or immoral acts (such as greed, theft, and sabotage of what is good). Don't pick up literature that sensationalizes what is immoral or illegal.
- **Let your friends know that you have a family policy of not watching programs or reading material that portrays evil and of**

not discussing it. Make it a point to avoid discussing evil activities or behaviors when children are present and refuse to allow your friends to discuss evil activities in front of your children.

- **Pray against evil in our society.**
- **Speak out against it.** Refrain from talking about the latest topic of sexual deviation discussed on the afternoon talk show. Refuse to be drawn into a titillating discussion about the details of certain immoral behaviors. Don't tell or listen to off-color jokes or stories.

   Turn the conversation to a more positive subject. If the others continue their topic, walk away or say to them, "I'd really rather not discuss this."
- **Don't dwell on it.** Thoughts about evil behaviors frequently result in dreams about them. Eventually you can become preoccupied with certain behaviors, which can lead to fear, to inner torment, and ultimately, if these thoughts are unchecked, to the act itself and its resultant guilt.

In most cases, you'll find that people are relieved to have the topic turned from evil toward good. There's less tension, less anxiety, less fear, and less discomfort. Also, if someone present has been a victim of evil, she may sense that she can trust you to share with her the grace, healing, and mercy of the Lord.

25 • In Talking About the Weather and the Scenery

Use your comments on the weather to point toward God's creation. Say, "What a day God has created!" Or, "Isn't this a beautiful day that the Lord has made? Let's rejoice and be glad in it!"

Is it raining? Say, "I hope the showers of blessing in your life are as nice as this spring rain!" Or, "You know, the Bible says that the rain falls on the just and the unjust. I'm glad I'm one of the 'just.'" Or, "It's a great day, isn't it, to be shut up with the Lord? I particularly enjoy studying my Bible on evenings like this."

Is the day a real scorcher? Say, "It's definitely hot enough to melt manna" (see Exod. 16:21). Or, "This day could cause us to want to avoid the heat of hell!"

Pointing Out the Beautiful Many people not only don't stop to smell the roses, they don't take time to look at them. Point out beauty to those around you. Take time to notice the landscape, the flowers, the trees, and the sunset. Again, point to the Creator. "Isn't it amazing how God's creativity never runs out?" Or, "Isn't this a fabulous display of God's love for us?" Or, "Aren't you glad that the Lord didn't make this a black-and-white world?"

- Call attention to the songs of birds and insects.
- Call attention to the variations of shape, texture, and color of the summer foliage.
- Call attention to the crocuses beginning to peep through the snowbanks.
- Call attention to the majesty of the mountains in the distance.
- Call attention to the flower growing out of the crack in the parking lot asphalt.
- Call attention to the variety in God's creation and the vast number of species and the beauty of mineral formations and precious and semiprecious stones.

In a utilitarian, function-oriented, human world, it's good to remind others that the Lord God is the original designer and engineer of this universe, the supreme artist and musician.

The Scriptures tell us that if we don't praise the Lord, even the stones will rise up and do so (see Luke 19:37–40). Let's not neglect the privilege that is ours of proclaiming the glory of the Lord wherever we see it!

26 • In Confronting Blasphemy

You can share your faith by not participating in blasphemy. In today's world, your lack of vulgar speech and profanity will stand out.

Speak Up When others use the Lord's name inappropriately in their conversations with you, don't remain silent. Speak up on behalf of your Friend of friends. When they use His name without courtesy, you might respond by saying sincerely and positively,

- "Excuse me, but you're talking about the most important Person in my life."
- "Yes, He's the One I'm living for."
- "I call Him Lord."
- "His name is truly higher than any other name on this earth."
- "Do you know personally the One you just called upon?"

All power in heaven and earth is given to the authority of the Lord Jesus Christ (see Matt. 28:18). When His name is used as a slang expression by someone who doesn't know Him or His power, His holy name is used in vain. If we let this misuse casually go by, our own perception of the power in His name could diminish.

Ways to Respond   When others say "God" as part of an angry phrase or as a swear word, respond,

- "God is, indeed, the One in whom I put all my trust to govern this world according to His standards."
- "God is my eternal heavenly Father, you know."

When you overhear profane and blasphemous phrases, ask the Lord to cleanse your mind and to keep them from staying in your memory. It's easy for us to repeat what we have heard before we think about it and to develop bad speech habits that can be very difficult to break.

When public figures use profane or blasphemous phrases, write them a note and express your desire that they be better role models for the children of our nation.

Let's honor the Lord in our speech—that the words of our mouths will be acceptable to Him (see Ps. 19:14).

27 • As You Travel

As you travel, consider yourself to be an agent of the Lord's peace, comfort, strength, and love in this needy world. Be an ambassador for Him wherever you go. Look and act as His emissary. Be on the alert for those who are in need around you.

Many people today are frightened as they travel.

- They may be fearful of flying, of being in a foreign land, of finding themselves alone in an unfamiliar city, or of being unsure of what to do or how to act.
- They may be going to or coming from emergency trips—perhaps to the bedsides of loved ones or to a funeral.
- They may be professional travelers—businessmen and businesswomen who are often weary of the world's pressures and the demands of their jobs.

You can be an agent of comfort, faith, and encouragement to such fellow travelers.

Pray Aloud If you encounter a violent storm or if the plane begins to bounce about as if out of control, try praying aloud,

God, save us. Put Your angels on the wings of this airplane and get us down safely!

Your fellow passengers may thank you for voicing the desire of their hearts!

Travel Together Many times the moments of fear in traveling are far less obvious. If travelers are not emotionally prepared for the unexpected crises that often accompany international travel, they can feel devastated or at a loss when those things happen.

If you see some distraught travelers, ask them if there is anything you can do to help them. If they indicate they'd like to talk, move to a quiet place and discuss their dilemma. Say to them simply, "Perhaps the Lord has something even better for you and your family." Invite them to join your group—they may be delighted to. The entire experience can turn into a great blessing.

Listen Travel in today's world is fraught with fear and unexpected crises, and delays are common as well. Has your trip been delayed? Look around—perhaps the delay is for a divine purpose.

If a fellow passenger seems to be in stress, use the time to listen to the other person's concerns. Express the confidence that we each can have in the Lord Jesus.

Until you reach heaven, you may never again see the person with whom God has trusted you to share His love. Therefore, it is important to encourage him to read the Bible, to talk to the Lord each day in prayer, and to find a church where he can grow in the grace and knowledge of the Lord and His Word.

28 • Using Tracts and Gospel Literature

Consider using elevators to distribute tracts. Elevators provide a captive audience—people who are generally silent and still for a few moments. You can use these few seconds to hand fellow elevator passengers a tract as you say, "You'll no doubt have a few moments while you're waiting for an appointment today, and here's something you may want to read while you wait. I think it might be of interest to you."

People will rarely turn you down, and they will often read what you have given them as they sit down in a hotel lobby to wait for an associate, wait for their breakfast to be served, have their shoes shined, or wait in an outer lobby for an appointment.

Sunday School Literature Don't throw away your children's Sunday school papers. Encourage your children to "recycle" them by giving them to their friends. These materials often present Bible stories as well as activities and puzzles related to the Bible. At times, your children may want to discuss the materials with their friends or to help them with the activities. Children in your neighborhood who don't attend Sunday school will be delighted to be given such a gift from your children.

Paperback Books In the news recently was a story about a man who left in hotels the paperback books he finished as he traveled. He had left a rather extensive paper trail on his international trips. Inside each book he wrote, "I hope you enjoy this book. When you are finished with it, pass it along to someone else." He included his name and home address, and he heard from appreciative travelers around the world.

The idea is a good one to adopt for Christ-centered books you read, particularly paperbacks that share personal testimonies. As you finish reading such a book, leave it where another person might pick it up—in a hotel room, a bus station, a dentist's lobby, or a seat on the subway. Who knows who might pick up the message about God's love that you leave behind. Rather than put your name and address in the book, consider leaving a note that says, "To know more, contact the church nearest you. The pastor will be delighted to tell you how you can know more about Jesus."

Remember as you share tracts and gospel literature with others that God grows the seeds we plant, even those we scatter or plant by the wayside. It is our responsibility to plant. It is His responsibility to use the seeds we plant for good in the lives of others.

29 • Being a Godparent

Accepting the request of a friend or close family member that you be the godparent of a child offers a unique opportunity for sharing your faith on repeated occasions, not only with the child but with others who see your relationship with the child.

- *As you buy meaningful spiritual gifts for your godchild, take advantage of the opportunity to share with the clerk who helps you.* Say, "This brass anchor is a graduation present for my godson. It's my heart's desire that he always have the Lord Jesus as his anchor."
- *As you talk about your godchild with others, let others know how you feel about the child.* "Having a godchild is one of the dearest relationships in the world." Share freely with your friends about how you felt the first time you walked with your godchild to the Communion rail. Talk about your godchild's personal decision to walk with the Lord. Share your godchild's bedtime prayers.
- *Ask the child's parents often about the spiritual life of the child you both love.* "How is my godchild doing spiritually? What should I be

praying about?" Your concern will touch the heart of the child's parents, and it could open up an opportunity for sharing about the Lord.

- *Pray for your godchild regularly.* Let your godchild hear you praying for her. Affirm her in prayer. "Thank You, Lord God, for the great privilege of knowing Mary and for loving her as my goddaughter."

- *As you talk directly to your godchild about the Lord, tell him what it means to you to be a godparent,* about the responsibility you feel for his spiritual life and about how you often pray for him.

- *Consider it your joy and privilege as a godparent to give your godchild a Bible* that he can read for himself. Inscribe it with your hope that he will read the Bible every day.

- *Feel free to share a passage of Scripture and stories of your own personal testimony with your godchild.* In talking about the Lord, you can say to your godchild, "I think the Lord would want me, as your godparent, to tell you this."

Take being a godparent seriously. Embrace the role. You'll have innumerable opportunities for sharing your faith.

Making a Public Statement

30 • Rent a Billboard

Millions of square feet in America are waiting to be redeemed with a positive message of faith. They line America's highways, its inner-city avenues, its rural roads. They are seen by millions of people a year. They cost less per message, per viewer, per unit than television or radio airtime and newspaper or magazine space.

What is this untapped resource for sharing the good news?

Billboards.

Check into the cost of billboard advertising in your city. Rent a billboard for a few months. You may be able to afford it alone, or join together with friends to display a public message of your faith. You may want to suggest that your church rent a billboard as a means of evangelistic outreach to your city.

Be Creative You may want to say simply, "Try God" or "God Cares," and give your church address or hotline telephone number. A church in Coalinga, California, has a billboard as you enter the city limits that reads: "Jesus is Lord of Coalinga."

Share Scripture   "The God of love and peace be with you—2 Corinthians 13:11," and add, "For more information, attend church."

Give a Personal Message

- "Thank God our son is now free from drugs."
- "Thank You, God, for bringing our child home!"

Or

- "We thank God for the birth of a miracle baby, Rachel."
- "Fifty years of marriage and we're still thanking God!"

Relate to Current Events   A friend was in Jerusalem recently and spotted a billboard that proclaimed, "The G-d of Israel is He that gives strength and power to His people. Psalm 68:35." Those in the area told him that the billboard had appeared shortly after Iraq's bombing of Israel during the Persian Gulf War.

Share Encouragement   "There's hope in the Lord." "God has a new supply of grace and mercy for you every morning." "In this unfaithful world, God's faithfulness toward you never changes."

Evoke Praise "God alone is worthy of worship." "Praise God. He's doing a great job given the circumstances we hand to Him!"

Invite People to Church "RSVP. We'd love to see you next Sunday at _____." Or feature a photograph of your church and say simply, "Saving Institution. Guaranteed Return."

Be sure to give your billboard readers an opportunity to respond to your message by giving a telephone number to call, the address of your church, or a post office box number.

31 • Write Your Leaders

We are challenged as Christians to pray for those who hold authority over us, both in the church and in our communities. One of the best ways to let your leaders know that you are praying for them is to write them.

Most public officials rarely receive notes of thanks or praise. Ninety percent or more of the correspondence from their constituents deals with complaints and problems. Your positive letter of encouragement is sure to stand out.

Make it a point this year to write a letter to the president, your senators, your representatives, your governor, your mayor, your councilperson, your police chief, the head of your local school board, or any other public official the Lord lays on your heart. Consider writing to the secretary of state, the secretary of defense, or members of the Supreme Court. Ask the Holy Spirit to direct you as you make a list of those you intend to write. You can get the names and addresses you need from your local library.

In writing:

- Affirm the individual as an important and valued person in your community or our nation.
- Let him know that you know he is valuable to God and that you believe he is holding his present office because God has entrusted him with this position of power.
- Tell her that you are praying for her as she undertakes the difficult, demanding job ahead of her. Let her know you are praying specifically for her health, family, safety, and wisdom in decision making.
- Share your concern for his eternal soul. Express your desire to see him in heaven someday.

You may want to add a verse of Scripture to your letter.

Write with respect and with compassion. Do all that you can to build up the person and cause her to want more of the power of God to be at work in and through her life.

Your letter doesn't need to be long. You can write very simply:

Dear _____,

I was compelled to write to you today to let you know that I appreciate you as my _____. You are valuable to God, and I want you to know that I am praying daily that you will have God's wisdom as you make the decisions so critical to the welfare of us all. I pray also for your safety and health and for the members of your family.

Above all, I pray that you may know the deep, abiding presence of God in your life and that you will live with the Lord forever in heaven.

Your sincere friend and constituent,

_____

You need not limit your letter writing to the leaders of our nation. You can be a one-person ambassador for the Lord and for our country in writing a positive, encouraging, Christ-centered letter to the leaders of other nations.

32 • Sing in the Park

Take a prayer walk through the park with some Christian friends. Sit in the park and begin to sing Christian choruses very softly to yourselves. Soon, people will probably stop to listen. Be prepared to answer questions such as "Why are you here?" and "What do your songs say?" Use the opportunity to share your faith and to give away Bibles. (Perhaps the women in your group can carry them in over-sized purses.) Let those gathered know that you are in the park simply to express Jesus' love.

Do you want to touch your community for Jesus this week? Do you want to share your faith with your neighborhood? Gather together a few Christian friends, tune up your guitars, and head for your local park this Sunday evening. Sing praises to the Lord. See what God will do with your sacrifice of song.

Your opportunities to sing about the Lord may have dramatic, far-reaching results. Who but God knows who will be in your audience, whose heart may be touched, and who may turn to the Lord?

Music has a way of reaching people as nothing else can. And when the heart is open, God's words are more readily received.

Campfire Singing   We have discovered in our years of Scouting that "The Battle Hymn of the Republic" is one of the most stirring songs that can be sung around an evening campfire. When sung with conviction, it is a song that can be—and has been—powerfully used by the Holy Spirit to bring conviction to the hearts of many.

Gifts of Music   Gifts of music are thoughtful and meaningful. Do you have friends who are leaving for a vacation by car? Consider sending along a praise tape as a bon voyage present. Traditional gospel songs or "spirituals" are welcomed by almost everyone.

In Times of Difficulty

33 • Pray for Discernment

Ask God to give you spiritual discernment. It is a gift He already has your name on. This gives you:

- the ability to see the need of another person as the Holy Spirit sees it,
- the ability to see what the Holy Spirit desires to do to meet the need in that person, and
- the ability to see how you may be used by the Holy Spirit in meeting the need.

For a Giving Heart Ask God to give you a loving, generous, giving heart. Ask Him to help you become less selfish and less self-centered.

Pray that God will make you a blessing. Ask God to speak through you and to act through you to help and comfort others.

For Others Next, pray for those with whom you come into contact daily. It may be the door-man at your office building or the child who sits across from you at your breakfast table. It may be the bus driver or your spouse. It may be the teacher of your course or your secretary. As you walk through your daily routine, pray silently for those you encounter. Look at people—*really* look at them. Look past their appearance, past what they are wearing, past their size and shape. See them as you believe the Lord sees them. What would He see about them that you usually would not notice?

To Be Used   In asking God to endow you with His discerning, loving heart, and in praying for others, you are truly putting yourself in a position to be used by God.

Ask the Lord for discernment. Ask for a loving heart. Ask to be made a blessing to others. He longs to answer those prayers.

34 • Pray for a Spiritual Birth

As you openly share your faith, you will no doubt experience times in which the person to whom you are talking is ready to take a major step in spiritual growth—to ask for and experience God's forgiveness and to enter into a personal relationship with the almighty living God.

Be prepared to pray with someone for a spiritual birth. Know how to lead in prayer.

If the Person Seems Hesitant to Pray

You may sense that the person is ready to accept Jesus Christ as her Savior and Lord yet is still hesitant about taking the step of confessing her sins and praying in your presence. Ask her if you can pray for her. If she is comfortable with that, pray that she will have the courage to ask God's forgiveness and that the enemy will not hinder her. Then, suggest that you lead her in a prayer that she can repeat after you, phrase by phrase. If she is willing to do so, pray with her a simple prayer that covers these five areas.

Prayer for a New Birth

First, help her recognize that God *is* and that He is the almighty One, the only God of the universe, the one true and living God.

Second, she should recognize that Jesus is God's Son, sent to this earth to show man how to have a living relationship with God our Father. Recognize that Jesus' death on the cross was the payment for the penalty of the sin that has separated her from God.

Third, she must admit the presence of sin and the absence of a relationship with God and face the consequences. Lead her to ask forgiveness for anything she has done that she knows is displeasing to God or contrary to His purposes.

Fourth, invite the Holy Spirit to come and live within her as the Spirit of Truth, the ever-present Counselor and Comforter who will lead her in the ways in which she should walk before God.

Fifth, lead the person to a make a commitment to live a Christian life.

A Sample Prayer   The prayer for a new birth need not be long or elaborate. It is the intent of a person's heart that is important. God always hears the words of a repentant heart. Here is a sample prayer:

God Almighty, Source of all that is, I come to You today recognizing I am a sinner. I am deeply sorry. I want to live in a way that is pleasing to You. I accept Your Son, Jesus Christ, and His sacrifice on the cross for the payment of my sins. Please wash me clean on the inside and remove everything that is displeasing to You. Please send the Holy Spirit to come and live within me, and to give me the strength to live a new life. I want to live the rest of my life serving and pleasing You. I ask this in the name of Jesus. Amen.

Leading a person into a new relationship with the Lord is one of the most exciting things you will ever do. Be bold in seizing every opportunity to help others experience the blessed relationship with Him that you enjoy and on which you have eternal hope and peace.

35 • At the Hospital

Persons in the hospital—experiencing pain, fearing the unknown, feeling the loneliness of an experience only they can know fully—are among the most open to receive encouraging words of faith.

- Share faith-building Scriptures with those you visit in the hospital.
- Give words of encouragement. Affirm the person's talents, personality, character, abilities.
- Speak and act as a person of peace. Let your voice be strong yet soothing. Give of your strength.

Your presence can mean a great deal to a sick friend or loved one. Recognize that to him you are the embodiment of the steadfast presence of the Lord.

Take this opportunity to ask him, "Are you satisfied with your relationship with God?" If he says, "No," ask if you can pray for him or with him. The prayer in number 34, "Pray for a Spiritual Birth," is an appropriate way to pray. Don't glibly assume that everything will be all right.

Don't Lose an Opportunity Frequently, you may have the opportunity to share with the loved ones of the person who is hospitalized. Perhaps you can sit in someone's place of vigil for a while so he can take a break. Perhaps you can go with him to the cafeteria for a moment of respite and conversation away from the hospital room. Be a good listener; let him set the tone and subject matter for your conversation.

Be sensitive to the Holy Spirit as to whether you should pray with a person before you leave her hospital room. You can always ask, "Would you like for me to pray for you?"

You may want to touch her or hold her hand as you pray. Pray believing that the Lord who hears your prayer is eager to answer your prayer and work on the behalf of the one who has been injured or who is ill. Pray for her total recovery—for her spirit, her mind, and her emotions as well as her body.

Above all, as you visit people who are hospitalized and greet their families, let them know that you are placing your trust in the Great Physician.

36 • In Financial Crisis or Loss

As you encounter those who are experiencing financial need—perhaps even bankruptcy or the loss of their businesses or jobs—assure them of three things that you believe:

1. God knows the need. He has not lost their name and address.

2. God is our Provider. He created all that is, He knows how to meet the need, and He has unlimited resources.

3. God has promised to meet our needs "according to His riches in Christ Jesus" (Phil. 4:19). He has entrusted to Jesus—and to the church—the means to meet needs.

Write a note of encouragement to a friend in need, expressing your beliefs and encouraging him to trust God as the Source of financial supply. As you write, remind him that his value as a person before God is eternal and that his financial worth has nothing to do with the worth of his soul.

Back to Basic Needs It is important to assure the person that God has promised to meet our *needs,* not our wants. God has not promised to provide every whim or to satisfy the lust of our eyes. He has promised to meet the basic needs of life—our need for food, water, shelter, clothing, and love.

Meeting Needs When You Can   At times, you may be in a position to share your faith best by meeting the financial or material needs of another person.

Bear in mind that most people who are experiencing financial trouble won't tell you they are. Ask the Holy Spirit to make you sensitive to those who are in need and to show you ways in which to help them.

Sharing your faith is always a costly commitment to our Master. He paid your eternal spiritual debt. In turn, you have the privilege of giving of your time, talents, and resources. God may ask you to meet the material or financial needs of others so that they will be more open to His greater blessings of eternal salvation with constant hope in the Savior. Don't ignore those opportunities when they come your way.

37 • In Grief

Perhaps the most valuable way to share your faith in times of grief is to "be there" with those who have lost family members. Your presence often conveys more than words can express. Just sitting in silent companionship with the bereaved family members expresses compassion.

Look for ways in which you can tangibly help the bereaved family:

- Pick up someone at the airport.
- Prepare a meal for them.
- Baby-sit a small child during the funeral.

If you are uncertain what to say to the bereaved, you can always say, "I love you. That's why I'm here."

In expressing your sorrow, avoid the tendency to say, "I know just how you feel." You probably don't. Every relationship differs; so, too, the sense of loss. What you can say is this:

I am praying for you in this time of loss. I know God is not only able but wants to help you through this time with victory in your soul.

The Homegoing of a Christian Family Member When a family member goes to be with the Lord, the event is a sad one for those who are left with her absence. You feel loss even though you know that your loss is heaven's gain. Your pain can be eased, however, if you will choose to take this opportunity to express your faith to others.

When someone dies, people are confronted with the fact that everyone will die someday. The comfort of faith is that this is a time of "sweet sorrow." Sorrow is real, and it is normal. The "sweetness" comes in knowing that heaven lies ahead. What has ended on earth has only begun in heaven. This is a time to invite others to prepare to meet their loved one in heaven by accepting forgiveness of sin from the Lord Jesus.

38 • In Breakups of Relationships

It is our privilege and our sacred responsibility to do whatever we can to keep a family together. But if the family does split apart, we must help mend the broken hearts of the individuals involved.

If you have a friend or loved one who is experiencing a broken heart through the breakup of a relationship, an engagement, a marriage, or a home, you can share your faith in vital ways:

Encourage Your Friend with Words from the Scriptures The prophet Isaiah tells us that the Lord Jesus was sent from heaven specifically to "heal the brokenhearted" and to "comfort those who mourn." He gives "beauty for ashes" and the "oil of joy for mourning." He gives "the garment of praise for the spirit of heaviness" (see Isa. 61:3). The woman mourning the end of a marriage should be ministered to by a Christian woman, and a Christian man should minister the Word to a deserted husband.

Jesus said of Himself that He had come to preach "deliverance to the captives" (Luke 4:18), including those held captive by memories of the past and a heart wounded in rejection.

Write notes of encouragement to a friend experiencing an emotional loss, pointing out to him who he is in the Lord and what the Lord desires for him to have and to experience. Point out his unique traits and special qualities.

Give Your Friend Words of Hope for the Future   When a heart breaks, it's easy for a person to conclude that the best of life is behind her and that all is lost. Point out that God is infinite and that He has an endless supply of good things still in store for her. Furthermore, He knows who she is, how she is made, what her needs are, where she lives, and how to care for her; and He values her beyond the ability of human words to convey.

Assure Your Friend that God Knows What Is Best for the Person who Hurt Him   Encourage your friend to forgive and to allow the Lord to deal with that person so that bitterness will not rule his emotions.

A spirit of unforgiveness or hatred reaps only unhealthy results for the person who refuses to forgive.

Take Time to Be with Your Wounded Friend   Call her just to say, "I'm thinking about you. How are you today?" Do things with her. Go places together. Invite her to come and bring her children to your family outings, to the park, to the library, to the museum, or to a holiday dinner.

Don't be afraid that divorce is contagious; it's

not. In fact, giving God's love to heal a broken heart will help you appreciate your own healthy marriage. And your friendship will help heal the void left in your friend's life.

Find Ways to Pamper Your Friend a Little Find out what she likes and indulge her. You'll be doing a great deal to help heal the wounds of rejection. If someone likes a special food, buy it for him or make it for him. If she likes a certain fragrance, buy bubble bath in that fragrance for her and offer to watch the children for an hour or two. If he's a fan of a particular team, buy an extra ticket so he can attend with your group.

Be aware of a tendency for your friend to become dependent on you. In helping him become whole again, always point to the Lord Jesus as the Source of his strength, his provision, his fulfillment, and his joy.

When their hearts are broken, many will seek solace in Jesus. Don't let them down. Lead them through a sinner's prayer and personally see that they are in a caring church group.

Creating
Celebrations

39 • Making Things Special

It is important that we honor one another. Romans 12:10 admonishes us, "Be kindly affectionate to one another with brotherly love, in honor giving preference to one another."

- *During times when others give awards or recognize the achievements of those you love, join in with hearty applause!* Be the biggest fan of those with whom you live, work, or associate.
- *At other times create awards or moments of recognition!* It is especially important to recognize the effort that a person has given to a task for which she has received no reward.

   It may be someone's first month without partaking of something to which he has become addicted. It may be the unheralded twelfth anniversary of employment.

   It may be the day that a couple pays the loan on the house in full. It may be the day a student passes a critical exam. Find excuses for celebration.
- *At still other times, you may need to honor a person simply because he needs to be recognized.* Perhaps he has never been singled out for

anything or has never achieved something that brought him noteworthy praise. His lack of public achievement doesn't negate his value as a fellow human being.

Host a celebration to honor the *person*— your celebration theme can always be "just for the joy of knowing you!"

Plan your celebrations with no hidden agendas. Don't honor a person in hopes that you will be recognized or that you will accomplish a personal goal. Honor others for *their* sakes, not your own!

Such celebrations build people up and create an atmosphere in which love flows freely. An abundant flow of love is contagious. It always attracts others toward the Source of your love, Jesus Christ.

In creating special events, do so with the thought that Jesus Himself will be in attendance. Use your very best of everything. Hold nothing back. Give it your all!

You are called to be a fountain of joy on this earth. May your celebrations overflow with His presence!

40 • Party Alternatives

In addition to the celebrations that you create as a Christian, you'll no doubt have many opportunities to share your faith at non-Christian parties.

Often the expression of your faith at a party will be in what you do not do more than in what you do. Refraining from vulgar language and telling wholesome jokes and stories will witness to a purity that is both compelling and convicting to many people.

Blessing over a Meal The hosts of large dinner gatherings frequently look for someone who can ask a blessing over the meal. Offer to do so. Pray, "We thank You, God, for providing such an abundance of food and for blessing us by letting us live in a nation where we are both free to produce and free to enjoy such abundance." After a few moments of silence, add, "Amen." Such a prayer is appropriate for most secular gatherings.

Promise Placecards Have you been asked to help with table decorations at a Scout function or a community banquet? You might want to include a "promise card" with a verse of Scripture at each table or even at each chair. You can buy such cards from just about any Christian bookstore or supply house.

An Alternative Party   At times you may want to host an alternative to a traditional secular party. Consider hosting a potluck "Hallelujah Party" rather than a Halloween party for your children and the families in your neighborhood. Invite the children to dress up as people who remind them of God. The children may come dressed as Bible heroes and heroines or as sports figures or as others the children know who have a strong Christian witness. The families will have a good time eating together and watching the children in their special "parade" through the house. Every child should win a prize. The party can speak to others of the way in which Christ Jesus is able to redeem every day of the year.

41 • Celebrating Spiritual Growth

Have a party! Join heaven in celebration when

- someone you know goes forward to make a commitment to Jesus Christ at the close of a church service.
- a young person makes a formal declaration of his faith in Christ.
- a new convert is baptized.
- someone announces her intention to engage in full-time ministry.
- a rebellious teenager publicly renews his or her faith.

Christian Decision Celebrate by inviting some Christian friends to join together for lunch after church at a local restaurant or country club, each family paying for its own meal. What a joyous occasion that can be—with various ones in the group praying blessings or sharing words of inspiration.

Infant Baptism or Dedication Often non-Christian family members will join you at church for the baptism or dedication of a baby even when they refuse your invitation at all other times. Turn such an occasion into a family celebration. Have a luncheon in your home with your minister after the dedication of a child. It can be a wonderful time to offer a round of "blessing" toasts to the infant, stating hopes for the child's life with the Lord Jesus on earth and throughout eternity. Share what a blessing it is to know the Lord. Above all, express Christian love toward the child and one another.

Let your family's unconditional love for a child who is being baptized or dedicated spill over to everyone there and soften the hearts of your unsaved loved ones toward Jesus our Lord.

42 • Bible-Style Celebrations

Use celebrations based on the Bible as opportunities to share their significance to you.

Passover Host a traditional Passover celebration, including a meal with authentic Passover foods. Share freely about the symbols associated with Passover, the scriptural basis for the celebration, and how Passover and Easter are related. This event could bring such depth of meaning to those who attend that it could become the first of many Passover meals you host.

If many questions are asked about the Bible, schedule more discussions. Your discussions could lead to regular Bible study.

Feast of Tabernacles You may want to invite your neighbors over for a Feast of Tabernacles meal. Read about that feast in the Bible and you'll get many ideas. You may want to build a traditional sukkoth, a booth, on your patio. How about a round-robin party with a potluck dinner at the home of a different family each night for the seven days of the feast?

Bible Foods   Host a children's lunch based on Bible foods, and invite the mothers of all your children's friends to attend. The refreshments can range from "bread of heaven" to cucumber and melon salad (see Num. 11:5). After lunch, have your children put on a puppet show that tells a Bible story for the rest of the children.

Celebrations based on the Bible can always be described as parties with a historical or cultural theme. Don't feel that you need to give a Bible study. Simply share what the event means to you as part of your faith in the Lord Jesus, and trust the Lord to quicken the spirits of your friends there to ask you more about His Word and His love.

43 • At Homecomings

Is a soldier in your family coming home from a tour of duty?

Is a student in your family coming home from college?

Is a family member coming home after being away for some time?

Celebrate the return!

It doesn't take a long time to prepare for a celebration. You'll be surprised at how much can be accomplished in an afternoon. In fact, you'll be amazed at how much you can do on your way to the airport to greet someone.

- Gather an armload of flowers.
- Blow up a dozen balloons. (Keep balloons on hand for spur-of-the-moment parties.)
- Make a quick sign or two. (It's also helpful to keep a roll of butcher paper or a few blank sheets of poster board on hand.)
- Stop and get a cake or several dozen cookies at the bakery. (You can even make the dough and bake the cookies during the party as part of the celebration.)

- Sing! "For he's a jolly good fellow" can easily be adapted to "jolly good student" or "jolly good cousin" or "jolly good Christian." If your loved one is a soldier, sing some patriotic songs.

It takes no planning at all to greet a loved one with open arms and lots of hugs.

Welcome Home from College Make a great deal of your children's return home for vacations. Invite friends and other family members to accompany you to the airport to welcome them home. This is an opportunity for new believers to see Christian love in action. It is an opportunity for your children to experience a firm foundation of community love and support for the decision they have made to attend a Christ-honoring college. Rent a room at the airport for a homecoming celebration—not only for your children but for the children of friends who may also be returning home the same evening. The feeling of belonging and love will lay a foundation of faith for these students.

Welcome Home from Vacation A wonderful way to show Christian love to a vacationing family is to welcome them home in a special way.

- Mow their yard for them.
- Plant flowers in an empty flower bed.
- Fix a homecoming meal so they won't need to

worry about cooking or shopping the minute they return home.
- Tuck little love notes into a basket of food you take to them.

Offer prayers of thanks for the safe return of your family members and friends. Thank the Lord for His mercy in bringing them safely back to you. Anticipate, too, the day when the open arms of loved ones will welcome you all to heaven.

44 • Remembering Your Spiritual Birthday

One of the best ways to share your faith is to have a party to celebrate your *spiritual* birthday—the day you were "born of the Spirit" as Jesus described to Nicodemus in John 3.

Feel free to host such a birthday party for yourself.

- Invite several friends over for tea.
- Invite friends to go with you for a game of golf.
- Invite friends to dinner.

During your celebration, let your guests know that you are celebrating a very important day—a spiritual birthday. However you celebrate, share with your guests the reason for your celebration and the ways you feel you have grown spiritually during the past year.

A Celebration to Remember One year, several women and I decided to attend a party across town, and although there were six of us and we knew we might be a bit cramped, we decided to ride together in one car. As we drove home, our conversation turned to stories of our spiritual birthdays, with several of us telling in detail how we had met the Lord Jesus and the wonderful changes in our lives since then.

One woman remained silent during this time, and she was the last person I dropped off at her home. She said to me, "I don't have a spiritual birthday, but I'd like to have one."

We all come into a spiritual birth in a similar way: we must leave our former lives, with all of the spiritual bondage and darkness of sin, and ask the Holy Spirit to breathe a newness of life into us, to link our human spirit with His, and to indwell us forever.

Invitation to New Birth I then told my friend how she could have a spiritual birth. I encouraged her to kneel by her bed and ask God to forgive her of anything she had ever done that she knew was displeasing to Him. I told her next to invite the Holy Spirit to come into her being to cleanse her and fill her with His presence. Her life was changed that afternoon.

In telling the story of your spiritual birth, you are likely to have the opportunity to lead another person into the same experience. Most of us are delighted to discover someone who shares our birthday. What a special delight when the birthday you share is a birthday in the Lord!

Moving into a Faith-Based Conversation

45 • "Is There Anyone Praying for You?"

My friend Judy and I were on our way home to southern California from a particularly exhausting trip to the East Coast. It seemed that every place we had gone, we had been drawn into deep spiritual discussions and intense spiritual counsel. While it was encouraging to see lives turn toward the Lord, the trip had been emotionally, mentally, physically, and spiritually exhausting.

On the flight home, we both settled in for what we hoped would be a restful sleep. Our secret wish was that the aisle seat next to me would remain open so we could spread out a little and relax. That was not to be. Down the aisle of the plane came our seatmate—a tall, unkempt young man with greasy hair and a black leather jacket. He carried a boom box, and his odor preceded his arrival.

If the Holy Spirit Arranges a Meeting

As he settled in, I introduced myself, which is my custom when I travel with others. I was surprised to see that this simple act of kindness and good manners shocked him. *He is accustomed to being shunned, not greeted,* I thought. The look in his eyes compelled me to ask, "Do you have someone in your life who is praying for you?"

He looked at me a little puzzled, so I explained. "If you do not have someone who is praying for you, and you aren't interested in knowing about the Lord Jesus, then I am going to sleep. But if you do have someone who is praying for you, then the Holy Spirit may have arranged our meeting today as a divine appointment, and I will stay awake to talk with you." His eyes welled with tears as he responded, "My grandmother is praying for me."

A New Energy All thought of sleep disappeared. The odor that had been so nauseating to both Judy and me was no longer noticeable. The exhaustion we had felt dissipated, and a new energy seemed to infuse us. We spent the rest of the flight talking with this man, who soon was crying openly. Before we landed, he had repented of his sins and entrusted his life to the Lord Jesus. An inner glow radiated from him.

"Do you have someone who is praying for you?" is a compelling question to those who are in rebellion against God. It calls them to confront what is truly important—and eternal. It reminds them of relationships that are dear to them, and it softens their hearts to the Holy Spirit.

If the Answer Is No What should you do if someone answers, "No"? Ask the Holy Spirit if this is a person for whom you should be praying. You may want to respond, "Then I will pray for you. Everybody should have at least one person who is praying for her."

46 • "I've Got Good News"

Most people are sometimes overwhelmed by bad news. Our media are filled with it—from talk shows to interview programs to prime time specials. We are frequently far more aware of what is bad or wrong in our world than what is good or right in it.

A Good Word A good word in a bad-news world can be an expression of your faith.

With enthusiasm in your voice, ask someone, "Do you know what good thing happened to me today?" Then share the most recent tender act of God's provision or love toward you.

Your "minitestimony" about what the Lord is doing for you—right now—is up-to-date evidence to those around you that God is still in control of this world and that He works in individual lives and circumstances.

- Point out ways in which the arm of the Lord has not been shortened.
- Give evidence to the fact that He can still reach into even the smallest of experiences and manifest Himself as our Deliverer.

At times, your good news might be an insight into God's Word or God's presence in your life. Say to someone, "I just had the most wonderful idea" or "I just figured out something." As you meditate on God's Word—reading it in the morning and carrying it with you in your thoughts all day long—you are likely to have new insights into the meaning of the Bible and to be more aware of God's working in and through you.

Share the News Share that "good news"! It may be the discovery that you are no longer attracted to something that had a negative pull on your life. It may be a new application of a verse in Proverbs. It may be the solution to a problem.

By sharing those insights with others, you are calling their attention to the fact that the Bible is the *living* Word of God and that it is the most relevant book ever written. You are witnessing to the fact that God operates now. He is both timely and eternal—both *now* and *forever*.

Be Encouraged Even if others don't fully understand your insight or comprehend why you consider something to be good news, they are likely to be captivated by your enthusiasm for the things of God.

Be encouraged! Even if others do not fully grasp the substance of your faith, you are sharing the reality of faith in your life.

47 • "You Are Important to the Lord"

Everybody wants to be important to somebody. That is the very basis for our sense of self-worth.

Frequently, however, people lose sight of their value.

- Perhaps they are receiving fewer compliments or rewards than they once did.
- Perhaps circumstances have turned against them.
- Perhaps they have never known unconditional love.

Regardless of what causes a loss of self-worth, the truth is that everyone is vitally and infinitely important to almighty God—in fact, we are so important to Him that He sent His only Son to die so that we might live with Him forever. You do well when you remind others of that truth.

A Measure of Faith God has given each person the ability to believe—most important, to believe that God is and that He wants to have a relationship with human beings. We all, therefore, have the ability to know God as our heavenly Father.

What a wonderful moment when a person truly embraces the fact that God chooses him to be His child and that He desires for him to have a loving, generous Father-child relationship with Him!

Unique Talents and Abilities   Each person has a wonderful, never-before-created set of abilities, talents, traits, background, and purpose on the earth. Each one is placed into a particular family in a particular nation during a particular period of time. Everyone is one of a kind in the human race. God has a specific need for each person to be on the earth and a specific purpose for each life.

- When you call a person's attention to her uniqueness, you are calling her to awareness that God has a plan for her life—a plan that is completely fulfilling and satisfying.
- In calling a person to a new or renewed awareness of God's love and to his unique creation, you will be activating his faith to believe God for something good in his life.

Several years ago, the early spring rains in Israel were so heavy that more wildflowers appeared than ever before in the history of modern Israel. Botanists even discovered some flowers that they had never seen before in the forty years since Israel became a nation. The seeds of those flowers had lain dormant in the scorching desert sun for decades.

Often the seeds of faith—which result in the harvest of a life's purpose—have lain dormant for decades, too. It takes the refreshing showers of the Holy Spirit's rain on the desert of a life to quicken the measure of faith within a heart.

Rain blessings on someone's faith today. Tell him how much God loves him and how important he is to Him. Remind her of the unique and wonderful way in which God has fashioned her. You won't extinguish anyone's faith in conveying this refreshing shower of blessings—rather, you'll cause faith to burst forth into full blossom.

48 • "What Do You See as the Foremost Problem Facing Our Nation Today?"

"What do you see as the number one problem we face today in our nation?"

Although you probably wouldn't begin a conversation this way, it is a question that can generally be asked as you continue talking with the person seated next to you on a train or an airplane, a person across the table from you at a business lunch, or a person sitting in a waiting room with you.

Listen closely to the answer. Probe the response.

- Why does she see this as the number one problem?
- How does she think the problem can be solved?
- What are the consequences she foresees if the problem isn't solved?

Personal Involvement Ask, "Are you involved in this problem in some way on a personal level?" If a person believes violence to be the most critical problem in our nation today, he may have experienced violence. He may respond with a story of physical or emotional abuse or with a story of having been the victim of a violent crime. *The broad needs and problems of society almost always have a direct correlation to individual needs and problems.* When you tap into that level of personal need, you are invariably touching a part of the person's life that bears upon his spirit.

When someone shares with you a personal story of tragedy, failure, need, or sorrow, you may want to ask if you can pray with him that God heal him of the memory or from the emotional pain of the experience.

Getting to the Answer As a person expounds upon the problem she perceives, look for ways in which you might move the conversation into spiritual concerns. You might say, for example, "I agree with you that this is a problem that is out of control, and it's virtually beyond human ability to unravel it. I'm grateful that the Lord God can see from the beginning to the end of this problem and that He will provide a way to solve it."

Or say, "It seems to me that this problem would not exist if people chose to live according to the Bible. Perhaps what we really need to do is call people back to a biblical way of living."

Most people know their needs, as individuals and as a society. Few know the One who is truly capable of meeting those needs. Count it a privilege and joy to share God's Answer, Jesus Christ.

49 • "What Is God Doing in Your Life?"

"What is God doing in your life?" is a question that calls someone to recognize God at work in him.

People to Ask This is an especially good question to ask new believers, churchgoers, or nominal or traditional Christians.

It is also a good question to ask around a campfire, at the close of a weekend retreat, or during a conversation with a Christian friend you haven't talked with in a while.

It's a good question to ask your teenager over a late night snack of milk and cookies. It's a good topic for quiet discussion with your spouse. If the person you ask hesitates in giving an answer, wait with empathy. Then, if the answer is not forthcoming,

- Volunteer your own answer. "Let me tell you what He is doing in my life. . . ."
- Point toward the changes in your life over the past six months, the year, or even the last ten years.
- Describe how you've grown in your understanding of God's Word during the past week.

- Tell of experiences that have strengthened your faith in God.

Sharing Faith Sharing your faith is certainly not limited to sharing your beliefs with non-Christians. You are called to share your faith continually with everyone, including those you call brothers and sisters in Christ. Often, God will place other Christians in your path so that you might encourage them and build them up.

In relating what the Lord is doing in your life—and in listening to what the Lord is doing in the lives of those around you—you become aware that your faith is shared with the body of Christ, with each member helping and building up the others.

50 • "Thank You, God!"

The psalmist tells you to enter the gates of our Lord's throne room with thanksgiving and to enter His courts with praise (see Ps. 100:4). To continually dwell in the presence of the Lord, then, is to continually be thanking and praising Him.

Joy One of the principal roles for a Christian is to be a wellspring of joy. Thanksgiving and praise are the manifestations of joy.

- Have you thanked God today for His blessings to you—appreciating what you have without resenting what you don't have?
- Do you acknowledge all of His good gifts to you with praise and adoration?
- Do you worship Him freely?

As good things happen to you, give thanks to God. Simply say, "Thank You, God!"

When someone compliments you on something you know was God's grace working in or through you, receive the compliment by saying sincerely, "Thank God."

In continually thanking and praising God for the good things in your life, you can do three things:

- *Call attention to the fact that God is a loving heavenly Father who desires the eternal best for all those who love Him and obey His commandments.* Thank God for your physical health and your material blessings, even as you thank Him continually for being your Savior and Lord.
- *Focus your attention on the good things of life rather than on evil.* Always recognize that a temptation to evil is deceiving—it is often disguised as attractive and beneficial. It takes a consistent effort to shun evil and concentrate on God.
- *Create a positive atmosphere around you in which conversations about the Lord Jesus are more likely to take place.*

Praise You may be fearful about what others will think or say and, hence, are silent—even when your heart is thankful or you feel like praising the Lord. If you are going to err, err on the side of being bold in your praise!

Let praise be your first, almost instinctive response to blessings as they come your way. Openly acknowledge the One who is the Source of everything you need, the Source of all inspiration and creativity, the Source of all energy and power. The Bible promises that if you will openly acknowledge Him before others now, He will openly acknowledge you before God.

51 • "Is There Something About Which I Can Pray?"

Nearly every person is aware of his own weakness or the greatest need or danger facing him. By asking someone, "How can I pray for you?" or "How would you like for me to pray?" you are opening up a deeper level of communication with that person. You are getting to the bedrock issues of his life, the issues that are closest to his eternal soul.

Relationship in the Spirit Furthermore, nearly every person that I have ever met was appreciative of prayer on his behalf. Prayer establishes a relationship in the Spirit that results in healing at many levels.

If a person responds, "Yes, I'd like you to pray," then by all means ask, "Shall we pray right now?" There's no time like the present when it comes to prayer. Even in the busiest, most public places of life, you can nearly always

- move to a more quiet out-of-the-way place.
- walk together, arm in arm, and pray aloud.
- pray for him as you take his hand, look into his eyes with the love of the Lord, and speak

words of encouragement, faith, and blessing as the Holy Spirit directs you.

(Don't limit your prayers to a particular place or posture or feel that you must close your eyes. Prayer is communication with God. It can and should happen anywhere and in any circumstance.)

Intercessory Prayer You will discover that as you pray for the needs of others, your heart will be turned toward those people. You will feel closer to them in the Spirit, and you will likely be more sensitive to them and more aware of their motives and God-given purposes on this earth.

Prayer is one of the most intimate ways in which you can help carry the burdens of others and bring about healing and wholeness in their lives and, in so doing, bring greater healing and wholeness to the entire body of Christ. Count it a privilege to pray for others. Make it an integral part of your daily walk with the Lord.

52 · "Tell Me Your Love Story"

Jesus said, "I have come that they may have life, and that they may have it more abundantly" (John 10:10). Jesus came to give us all good things in quantities greater than we could contain them—including His joy, His peace and, above all, His immeasurable love.

Sharing Love Stories Some of the most interesting and enjoyable conversations I have ever experienced have involved the sharing of love stories—hearing how God has brought two people together into a loving relationship, discovering ways in which their love has grown through the years, and witnessing how tender and kind even gruff or cold people can become when they tell how they fell in love.

- Love stories bring out dear emotions in everyone.
- They remind people of their need for love and how wonderful it is to experience love.
- Remembering these emotions builds strength in a marriage.

As you share love stories with others, you'll find it easy to move gently into sharing the greatest love story of all time, that of the Father sending His Son to this earth to show that His love is more tender, more lasting, and more intimate than any human love can ever be.

God's love is without manipulation, without jealousy, without constraints, and without conditions. It flows freely and is available to all. Experiencing His ever-present love causes humans to want to live in His holiness and to continually share their faith with others.

Faith Walk In sharing your faith, you are actually inviting people to fall in love with Jesus and to do so more and more each day of their lives. The wonderful fact of a faith walk is this:

- The closer we follow Him and the more we communicate with Him, the more we experience His presence and the deeper our relationship with Him grows.
- The deeper our relationship, the greater our love for Him.
- The more we love Him, the more we realize that He loved us first.
- The more we comprehend His love for us, the more we realize that we can never comprehend it fully or encompass it all. His love is overflowing and omnipresent.

In sharing your faith, you are actually inviting people to receive His abundant life and to experience His abundant love for themselves. No greater invitation can ever be offered to anyone!

Invite someone today to be part of the greatest love story ever told. That person will thank you eternally.